THE REVENGE BOOK

by

BOB SMITH

INTERIOR LINE ART BY B. BENJAMIN

PUBLISHED BY PALADIN PRESS, BOULDER, COLORADO

"One should always 'get even' in some way, else the sore place will go on hurting."

Mark Twain
A Tramp Abroad

TABLE OF CONTENTS

INTRODUCTION . . . 1

CHAPTER ONE: ATTACKING
ON THE HOME FRONT . . . 13
EVIL EYE . . . PHONEY PHONE-IN . . . PARTY LINES . . .
EARBENDERS . . . BLACKOUT . . . HOUNDED AND
IMPOUNDED . . . LOST WEEKEND . . . PHILANTHRO-
PISSED OFF . . . FOOD FOR THOUGHT . . . FUTURE
SHOCK . . . CALLING ALL CURS . . . TRICK-OF-THE-
MONTH . . . NOWHERESVILLE, U.S.A. . . . SLICK
TRICK . . . WELL DUN . . . VICAR-IOUS VISIT . . .
MANURE CURE . . . TERMINAL TAXIS . . . ANTS FROM AN
UNCLE . . . DEFOLIANTICS . . . TWO-FISTED UNLISTED
. . . AD IRRITATUM

CHAPTER TWO: SHATTERING ALLIANCES . . . 27
PHONE PHUN . . . SEPTIC SHENANIGANS . . . RESERVA-
TIONS FOR TWO . . . BRIEF MESSAGE . . . POSTAL
PARANOIA . . . THE PHANTOM JEWELER . . . KINGSTOWN
SALLIE . . . KNOW THIS MAN? . . . A ROSE BY ANOTHER
NAME . . . MONEYGRAM SCAM . . . TAPPED RESOURCES
. . . HIGH HEELED SNEAKY . . . POSTAL PERFIDY . . .
REDECORATE . . . RUBBER PLANT . . . MAIL LUST . . .
HAVANA AFFAIR . . . LOW RENT RENDEZVOUS

CHAPTER THREE: PERSONAL COMBAT . . . 43
HAPPY BIRTHDAY . . . TERMINAL CANCEL . . . BOSS
SLUR . . . STAND BY . . . INFERIORITY COMPLEX . . .
ELEVEN MOST WANTED LIST . . . DEADBEAT . . .

VOODOO ADIEU . . . NERVOUS SERVICE . . . ERROR
PARENT . . . HOT PLASTIC . . . ROADSIDE ATTRACTIONS
. . . SECRET STORM . . . HOLIDAY SPIRIT . . . MAIL
ODOR . . . NO SALE . . . CHECKUP SETUP . . . ALL WORK
AND NO PLAY . . . AYE, THERE'S THE RUB . . . HANGING
ON THE TELEPHONE

CHAPTER FOUR: TAKING THE FIGHT TO THE STREETS . . . 55

GAY BARB . . . GHOST WRITER . . . FUNEREAL FUN . . .
A.P.B. . . . BADMOUTH . . . PERVERT ALERT . . . DOOR
TO DOOR DILEMMA . . . MANLY MISCHIEF . . . PAINT IT
BLACK . . . HIT AND MISSIVE . . . TO CATCH A THIEF
. . . OUT TO LUNCH . . . MINOR INCIDENT . . . BRAT
CHAT . . . SICK CALL . . . SPYMASTER (BAITER) . . .
COMPANY MAN . . . WHILE YOU WERE AWAY . . .
BOSSITIS . . . HIRE THE EX-CON . . . EXECUTIVE ACTION
. . . LOUSE OF ILL-REPUTE . . . MYSTERIOUS MES-
SAGES . . . LETTER BOMBAST . . . FALSE ALARM . . .
$B^3 = 0$ . . . STOOD UP

CHAPTER FIVE: BRINGING UP THE HEAVY ARTILLERY . . . 71

TAXING PROBLEMS . . . THINK PINK . . . PAPER MURDER
. . . UNWILLING ACTIVIST . . . JUST A CONCERNED
CITIZEN . . . FRIENDLY NEIGHBORHOOD PUSHER . . .
SYPHILITIC CRITIC . . . AGRICULTURAL AID . . . ABUSE
RUSE . . . MOONLIGHTER . . . SWEET DREAMS . . .
ASININE PROBE . . . GUERRILLA WARFARE

INTRODUCTION

What would you do if the office backstabber zeroed in on you—and you lost your job as a result?

What would you do if your boss deliberately humiliated you in front of people you respect?

What would you do if a 275-pound palooka battered you to a pulp just to show off for his girl friend—then walked away scot-free because she testified you started the fight, and you had no witnesses?

If you're like most people, you would do nothing.

Revenge has become something most Americans don't even consider. When we're wronged, we stew inside but passively accept it. We have become, literally, a shameful nation of sheep . . . and that's a sad commentary on the state of America today.

Can you imagine our American ancestors letting anyone do them dirty? Not on your life! Back in the good old days, personal revenge was a personal matter. If somebody screwed you, you asked him outside to settle the score with guns, fists, or whatever else was handy.

Today, sad to say, things are not that simple. Our complex, law-ridden society has effectively stifled the spirit of revenge in most people by lowering the boom

1

on anyone who tries to get even through those old, time-honored methods of personal attack.

As a result, people are getting royally screwed all the time, and they do nothing about it.

Bill Daniels was an easygoing kind of guy, the kind who liked to help people. If somebody needed a small loan, he could always be counted on to provide it. If a neighbor wanted to borrow his lawn mower, he was happy to oblige.

One morning Bill was driving to work in his battered old pickup truck, drinking a beer for breakfast, when suddenly a car ran a red light and banged into his fender. The other driver jumped out and looked at the damage with worry etched on his face.

"Listen, mister," the other fellow pleaded, "I don't have a bit of insurance. If we call the cops, they're going to jail me sure as hell. Can't we just settle this right on the spot and leave the police out of it? I've got a little cash . . ."

Bill studied the dent in his truck, then checked the damage to the car. He rubbed his chin.

"Tell you what," he said finally, "let's just forget it. This old truck of mine isn't worth fixing, and your car isn't damaged that much. No use bothering the cops and my insurance company."

The man's face brightened and he stuck out his hand. "Hey, thanks! I sure appreciate it," he said, pumping Bill's hand.

Bill cruised away, sipping his Schlitz and feeling good inside. He'd done his good deed for the day.

He drove eight blocks before police pulled him over and arrested him for leaving the scene of an accident and running a red light. They had been called by the other driver.

Bill had to pay a bondsman $50 to get him out of jail, plus $100 to an attorney to represent him in court. He was convicted of both charges, thanks to the testimony of a passenger in the other man's car, and was fined $150. Bill also had to pay $200 to fix the man's auto. Then the guy sued him, claiming a whiplash injury, and Bill shelled out another $1,500 in attorney fees, court costs and judgments.

Total cost of Bill's "good deed": over $2,000, nearly a fourth of one year's take-home pay.

For six months after her divorce, Becky Townsend had searched for a good apartment. Finally, to her delight, she found one that was not only reasonably priced, but close to the restaurant where she worked as a waitress. In addition, there were plenty of children with whom her four-year-old son, Chad, could play.

Two weeks after moving in, Becky decided to treat herself to a night on the town. She ended up at a local bar, and soon found herself talking with a roughly handsome, muscular young man named Frank.

As the conversation progressed, however, Frank's language became more and more offensive. Finally, Becky excused herself and walked out. She drove to her mother's home, picked up Chad, and returned to her apartment. As she was turning the key in her lock, she felt a hand on her shoulder.

Becky whirled in fright. It was Frank. He had followed her home.

"What are you *doing* here?" Becky asked angrily.

Frank smiled. "Hey, baby," he said, "I'm just not through talking to you yet, that's all."

"Well, I'm through seeing *you*. Now please leave!"

He leaned against the wall. "I'm not going anywhere until I get a nightcap. Gotta have a drink, understand? I'm staying right here until you invite me in."

Becky's gaze was withering. "No," she said firmly.

Frank's voice rose. "Then I guess I'll have to ask one of your neighbors for a drink." He turned toward the door opposite Becky's and said loudly:

"Hey, anybody in there got a drink? I'm dying of thirst out here."

Becky was frantic. She did not want her new neighbors mad at her. She hesitated, torn by indecision. Frank yelled again.

"Oh, all right!" said Becky. "But just one drink and then I want you out of my apartment."

"Just one drink. I promise," said Frank.

He followed her inside. As she fixed his drink, Frank excused himself and went to the bathroom. When he came out, Becky almost dropped the glass. He was stark naked.

"Come on, let's screw," he said, rotating his hips suggestively.

Becky slammed down the glass. "Get out of my apartment!" she yelled. "You filthy, disgusting man!"

"Get out or I'll call the police!"

"What are you going to tell them? That I broke into your apartment? It's obvious I didn't." He rubbed his genitals and grinned again.

Becky was stalemated. She couldn't call the cops, that would create a terrible scene. She didn't dare wake a neighbor to ask for help. And she couldn't walk out and leave Frank alone in her apartment. Besides, there was little Chad to worry about.

It was a long, exhausting night. Finally, just before dawn, Becky's ordeal ended when Frank gave up and left.

But that was only the beginning. Frank started coming to her apartment at all hours of the night, banging on the door and demanding she let him in. After four weeks of this, Becky's landlord told her he was sorry, but she would have to move.

So Becky lost the best apartment she'd ever had. In the weeks that followed, she learned that her tormentor was a loan clerk at a local bank, who had a wife and three children, and taught Sunday school class. Becky wished fervently she could put the fear of God into him, but she just didn't know how.

When Steven Richards bought his house, he knew water frequently seeped into the basement. He had planned to seal the walls, stop the leaking once and for all. Before he got around to it, Steve was offered a better job in another town and decided to take it.

He and his wife listed their house with a realtor named Barney Jacobs, who had a reputation for moving property fast. Only hours later, Barney was knocking on their front door with a well-dressed, middle-aged couple in tow.

"Walter and Martha Wagner," Barney announced, sweeping into the home. "They'd like to look over your house." He steered the Wagners toward the kitchen. Steve, taken aback, was angered by the sudden intrusion but said nothing.

They reached the den. Barney pointed to a trapdoor in the parquet floor. "That lead to the basement?" he asked. Steve nodded, and the realtor lifted the door. He started down the stairs.

"Careful," said Steve. "There's no light down there. We don't use that area—it's only a partial basement, really, just six by eight feet—and there's usually some water seepage in it."

"Yeah," said Barney, his voice sounding hollow in the stairwell. "There's a couple of inches on the floor right now." He came stomping back up the stairs and made wet prints across the floor as he and the Wagners looked through the rest of the house. Steve's wife frowned her displeasure, but kept quiet until the three left.

That night Barney returned alone. "Well, they're interested in the place," he said, "but Mr. Wagner's worried about that leaky basement. He says if you'll knock $500 off the purchase price, he'll buy the house and use the $500 to seal the basement walls."

"Five hundred dollars—to seal a basement?" said Steve incredulously. "Why, anybody knows you can get the job done for two hundred."

Barney shrugged. "Sorry, but that's his best offer. And to tell you the truth, I don't think you'll get a better one from anybody."

The realtor's persuasiveness finally swayed Steve and his wife. They sold at the lower price.

One year later, Steve got a registered letter informing him the Wagners had filed suit against him for $10,000, claiming the basement had leaked and damaged their home. They charged that the basement was dry when they bought the house, and that Steve had given them an oral guarantee it had never leaked and never would.

Steve was thunderstruck. He called his lawyer. "How can they sue?" he asked. "They knew the basement leaked, and I even knocked $500 off the price so Wagner could get it fixed."

"Well, they're claiming otherwise," said his attorney. "And if you don't file an answer to their suit, they'll win automatically."

Steve called Barney. "What's going on?" he asked. "Why didn't Wagner take that $500 and get the basement sealed?"

"Five hundred dollars?" asked Barney. "What five hundred dollars?"

"Why, the five hundred dollars I knocked off the price!"

Barney's voice held just the proper tone of perplexity. "I'm sorry, old buddy, but I don't remember you knocking anything off the price. And as I recall, the basement *was* dry when they bought the house."

With a sinking feeling, Steve realized he'd just been screwed.

He had no choice but to file an answer to the suit. And with Barney slated to testify against him, Steve had to settle out of court. It wasn't much—four hundred dollars—but the attorney's fees, court costs, and trips back to his former home town brought Steve's bill to $1,400.

Later, Steve learned from Barney's ex-partner that Barney and Wagner were old friends, that Wagner had asked the realtor to find him a home in the neighborhood, and that the two often joked about ripping off Steve.

But the ex-partner refused to testify in court to those facts, saying he didn't want to get involved. Steve could only swallow his anger.

All of the above stories are true (the names, of course, have been changed for legal reasons) and they vividly illustrate the painful fact that it is easy for somebody to give you the shaft, yet incredibly tough for you to strike back without getting hassled.

These days, most people do not seek revenge for three main reasons:

(1) *Money*. They can't afford to sue the person who has wronged them, or just don't want to risk their hard-earned cash.

(2) *Time*. Lawsuits mean days and even weeks lost from work, with a resulting loss of income. And there is never a guarantee of winning the suit.

(3) *Legal hazards.* If they commit a serious crime (like assault or arson) while getting even, they could easily go to jail or get sued.

The result? When most people get screwed, they simply grin and bear it.

Few Americans have the guts to do as a West Palm Beach, Florida man did recently. Harassed by a neighbor, he lured the man to a lonely swamp area, tied him to a tree—and left him for the alligators (the man got away).

Most people, in fact, won't even go as far as a New York man did. Ordered to pay alimony to his ex-wife even though she was making more money than he, the man made each monthly payment in pennies—stuffed inside jars of molasses. It took months for his exasperated ex to get a court order forcing him to stop.

But there *are* ways of getting even without resorting to violence, risking a prison stay, or even letting the guy (or gal) know you're the one after him. This book gives you tips on how to do it. You might have to spend a few bucks in the process, but it'll be a drop in the bucket compared to the enormous costs you would incur if you filed a lawsuit against your enemy. And you'll get an excellent return on your dollar. In terms of personal satisfaction, there is no better investment than revenge.

But just as a tiger waits with infinite patience for its victim *you* must wait a respectable time before you start to get even. If you begin too soon after you've been wronged, your enemy will know immediately who is after him. But if you wait—say, a year—he will assume you have forgotten about the wrongdoing. And chances are that he'll wrong other people during that year, so *they* will become his chief suspects instead of you.

What do you do during that year? Find out all you can about the victim. Follow him. Watch him. Know his every move. To be successful, vengeance—as with any worthy undertaking—must be well-planned, and if you know your enemy intimately, you will have a tremendous edge on him. Learn his spouse's name and the names of close relatives like brothers and aunts. Learn his phone number, both at home and at work, and his home address. If he has a post office box, find out the number. Draw up a detailed list of his habits, perversions, likes and dislikes. Find out exactly what he does for a living, and who his superiors are. If possible, get his social security and charge card numbers. Learn his hobbies and regular activities such as Friday night bowling or vacations each August. Obtain a sample of the victim's handwriting from his office wastebasket or the garbage cans outside his home.

It isn't really that tough to get information about people. For example, if the victim has an unlisted number, go to your local library and find his name in the city directory (it often lists unlisted numbers). If that doesn't work, call the victim's mother (or other close relative) and say you must get in touch with your old friend, her son, right away but have misplaced his phone number. Nine times out of ten she will give it to you.

If you live or work near the victim, this gives you tremendous advantages in planning and carrying out your revenge. You will be able to learn helpful bits of information about him; observe his habits and schedules; and be in a position to act quickly when a chance for vengeance arises.

When the waiting period is over and you put your plan of revenge into action, here are some things to remember:

(1) Fit the punishment to the crime. Strike back with a severity equal to the offense against you—or as the Bible notes: "an eye for an eye."

9

(2) Be sure to wipe your fingerprints off anything you mail, or off anything at all that will ultimately end up in the victim's hands. To keep fingerprints to a minimum, wear a pair of cheap rubber gloves while handling things.

(3) In some cases, especially if your victim knows your voice, you will need the help of a trusted accomplice. This can be a close friend, your spouse or another relative, or a stranger who needs a couple of bucks. You will find that after you tell people how the person has wronged you, they'll share your outrage and gladly help.

(4) Always use a pay phone. If your victim has complained to authorities about receiving harassing calls, it *is* possible they might put a tracer on his line. New electronic gadgetry developed by the telephone company reportedly pinpoints the source of a call in seconds. No more of that "keep him talking until we can trace the call" stuff you see on TV.

People tend to accept phone calls as authentic if they hear appropriate background sounds. If, for example, they're getting a call from Western Union, they expect to hear chattering teletype keys and bells going "ding-ding." If the caller says he's at home, they expect to hear a TV set or children in the background.

So you must provide these background sounds, even if you are calling from a pay phone. To do this, record the sounds on a small tape recorder and play them back as you make the call.

Letters, too, must appear authentic. If your letter purports to be from a motel, it must have a motel letterhead. The same goes for companies, department stores, and other places.

To obtain letterheads from companies or stores, simply write them about job opportunities, complaining about an item you bought, etc. When they reply, clip off the letterhead at the first fold and attach it to the top of the letter you are sending to the victim (or to his wife, boss). Xerox the combination and mail the copy.

You can get stationery bearing motel and hotel letterheads just by raiding the desk drawers when you check into one of these places. Most provide free stationery.

Do not expect all of the tips in this book to work all the time. Whether or not they will work depends on a number of factors including the character of your enemy and other people with whom you'll be dealing, your ability to project sincerity over the phone and in the letters, and the amount of preparation you put into each project. But many of the ideas in this book have proven extremely effective in actual practice.

As you move through the book, you will notice that some of the ideas take a little nerve to carry through to conclusion. But keep in mind the immense satisfaction you'll feel in getting even. You will no longer feel like a whipped dog. You will have regained pride in yourself, and your enemy will have met his just desserts.

Another thing: if you're a woman, don't think you can't get even, too. Men don't have a monopoly on vengeance —in fact, women get screwed (figuratively speaking) as often as men in today's society.

As you watch the victim squirm, you'll be tempted to let him know—or at least hint to him—that you're his tormentor. Don't do it. Here's why:

(1) He could strike back. Many of the ideas suggested in this book could make him furious enough to physically attack you.

(2) If he knows who is after him, it removes some of the fear you've built up. Far better to let him view his adversary as a nameless, faceless being, a shadowy figure skulking somewhere out there in the dark. The victim

11

won't know how far this sinister mystery man will go in wreaking revenge because he has no idea why the person is after him.

When you go for revenge, *do not feel sorry for your victim.* He is, after all, the person who screwed you without mercy, and therefore deserves the same treatment.

Use every means at your disposal to strike back. As Nietzsche points out, when it comes to getting even, "no means are too venomous, too underhand, too underground and too petty."

Good hunting.

CHAPTER ONE
ATTACKING ON
THE HOME FRONT

EVIL EYE

CUT A GIGANTIC EYE OUT OF A MAGAZINE, PASTE IT ONTO A SHEET OF PAPER, AND MAIL IT TO YOUR VICTIM. THIS WILL SERVE AS HIS FIRST HINT THAT SOMEONE IS WATCHING HIM.

PHONEY PHONE-IN

PHONE A RADIO TALK SHOW—MOST OF THESE LET THE CALLER SELECT HIS OWN SUBJECT—AND SPEAK OUT ON A CONTROVERSIAL SUBJECT. BUT CHOOSE THE LEAST POPULAR SIDE. IF MOST OF THE CITY IS BITTERLY AGAINST FORCED BUSING, FOR EXAMPLE, SAY YOU'RE FOR IT. IF FACTORY WORKERS ARE OUT ON STRIKE, VERBALLY ATTACK THE STRIKERS AS ''UNION-CONTROLLED ZOMBIES.'' GIVE THE VICTIM'S NAME AND ADDRESS.

IF YOU'RE AFRAID YOUR VOICE WILL BE RECOGNIZED, GET A PAL TO PHONE FOR YOU.

PARTY LINES

SEND OUT 200 INVITATIONS TO A BARBECUE PARTY AT THE VICTIM'S HOME. TO MAKE IT APPEAR MORE AUTHENTIC, ASK GUESTS TO "BRING YOUR OWN BOTTLE."

EVEN IF THE VICTIM LEARNS OF THE HOAX SEVERAL DAYS BEFORE GUESTS START ARRIV- ING AT HIS HOME, HE'LL NEVER BE ABLE TO LET ALL OF THEM KNOW THERE'S NO PARTY— BECAUSE HE WON'T KNOW WHOM YOU'VE INVITED. YOU MIGHT EVEN INVITE YOURSELF.

IF THE VICTIM IS HAVING A PARTY AND YOU KNOW THE TIME:

1. CALL THE POLICE AND COMPLAIN THE PARTY IS TOO LOUD.
2. PHONE HIS NEIGHBORS, SAY YOU'RE ONE OF HIS GUESTS, AND INVITE THEM ALL TO THE PARTY.

EAR BENDERS

SEND THE FOLLOWING PEOPLE TO THE VICTIM'S HOME:

1. ENCYCLOPEDIA SALESPEOPLE.
2. COSMETICS SALESPEOPLE.
3. VACUUM CLEANER SALESPEOPLE.
4. CORRESPONDENCE SCHOOL REPRESENTA-TIVES.
5. INTERIOR DECORATORS.
6. CARPET SALESPEOPLE.
7. INSURANCE PEDDLERS.
8. MAGAZINE SALESPEOPLE.
9. FERVENT SALVATION SELLERS.
10. ROOFERS, PAINTERS, AND OTHER HOME REPAIR PEOPLE.
11. BURIAL PLOT SALESPEOPLE.
12. REALTORS—TO APPRAISE HIS HOME FOR A SALE.
13. CHARITIES TO PICK UP "DONATED" CLOTH-ING, FURNITURE, ETC.

BLACKOUT

CALL THE TELEPHONE, WATER, AND POWER COMPANIES, GIVE THE VICTIM'S NAME AND SAY YOU WOULD LIKE YOUR SERVICE DISCONTINUED BECAUSE YOU ARE MOVING OUT OF TOWN. GIVE THEM A FAKE FORWARDING ADDRESS AND TELL THEM TO SEND YOUR FINAL BILL THERE. IF YOU DO THIS ON A FRIDAY, THE VICTIM CAN'T GET HIS SERVICE RESUMED UNTIL AT LEAST MONDAY.

HOUNDED AND IMPOUNDED

IF THE VICTIM'S PET DOG OR CAT DOESN'T WEAR A COLLAR, CALL THE CITY POUND AND ASK THEM TO PICK UP THE "STRAY." TELL HIM IT'S ACTING RABID, AND YOU'RE AFRAID IT'LL ATTACK ONE OF YOUR KIDS.

LOST WEEKEND

IF THE VICTIM AND HIS FAMILY LEAVE TOWN FOR THE WEEKEND:

(1) CALL A LANDSCAPING FIRM OR TREE SUR-GEON AND TELL THEM TO REMOVE A LARGE TREE FROM HIS YARD, EXPLAINING THAT IT IS DISEASED OR IS BLOCKING YOUR VIEW.

(2) SEND OVER A LAWN SERVICE TO CUT HIS GRASS, TRIM HIS HEDGES, AND SEND HIM A BIG BILL.

(3) GET A PEST CONTROL SERVICE TO SPRAY THE EXTERIOR OF HIS HOME FOR ANTS AND TERMITES.

(4) LEAVE A NOTE ON HIS FRONT DOOR SAYING: ''HI, SWEETIE. STOPPED BY AGAIN BUT ALL WAS DARK SO I DIDN'T KNOCK. BETTER CALL ME RIGHT AWAY—WE HAVE SOMETHING IMPORTANT TO DIS-CUSS.'' THE NOTE SHOULD BE UNSIGNED BUT IN A FEMININE HAND, AND PROMINENTLY DISPLAYED.

(5) ORDER A LOAD OF LUMBER AND GIVE THE VICTIM'S ADDRESS.

(6) GO TO A SAND AND GRAVEL COMPANY, PAY FOR A TRUCKLOAD OF GRAVEL ($20-$25) AND HAVE IT DUMPED: (A) IN THE VICTIM'S FLOWERBEDS; (B) ALL OVER HIS LAWN; (C) ON HIS FRONT PORCH.

PHILANTHROPISSED OFF

ANY TIME YOU'RE WATCHING A CHARITY TELE-
THON OR POLITICAL FUND-RAISING SHOW, PHONE
IN A PLEDGE IN THE VICTIM'S NAME. THEY'LL BUG
HIM FOR MONTHS TO PAY UP.

SIMILARLY, ANY TIME YOU SEE A TV AD IN
WHICH THE EMCEE SAYS: ''CALL THIS TOLL-FREE
NUMBER NOW—OPERATORS ARE STANDING BY!''
CALL AND ORDER THE PRODUCT IN THE VICTIM'S
NAME. HE'LL GO CRAZY TRYING TO STOP THE
FLOOD OF ITEMS.

IF THE VICTIM'S CHURCH IS HAVING A CHARITY
DRIVE, CALL AND MAKE A LARGE PLEDGE IN HIS
NAME.

FOOD FOR THOUGHT

CALL RESTAURANTS SPECIALIZING IN CHINESE,
MEXICAN, AND ITALIAN FOOD, AND HAVE THEM
DELIVER ORDERS TO THE VICTIM'S HOME
SIMULTANEOUSLY.

FUTURE SHOCK

ANY TIME YOU SEE A NEWSPAPER OR MAGAZINE AD WHICH LETS YOU ORDER ANYTHING COD OR "BILL ME LATER," DO IT—IN THE VICTIM'S NAME.

IT'S BEST TO SEND HIM MATERIAL THAT IS OBJECTIONABLE TO HIM. FOR EXAMPLE, IF HE'S A VEGETARIAN, ORDER A COUNTRY HAM.

CALLING ALL CURS

CALL THE LOCAL RADIO STATION, AND IN A CONCERNED VOICE REPORT THAT YOUR DAUGHTER HAS LOST HER BELOVED DOG. ASK THE STATION TO BROADCAST A DESCRIPTION OF THE ANIMAL, PLUS THE ANNOUNCEMENT THAT YOU'RE OFFERING A $50 REWARD FOR ITS RETURN. GIVE A VAGUE DESCRIPTION WHICH COULD MATCH A THOUSAND STRAY DOGS, AND ASK THAT ANYONE FINDING THE ANIMAL BRING IT TO YOUR HOME. GIVE THE VICTIM'S ADDRESS.

TRICK-OF-THE-MONTH

SIGN THE VICTIM UP FOR THE "BOOK-OF-THE-MONTH," "RECORD-OF-THE-MONTH," OR ANY OTHER CLUBS WHICH SHIP ITEMS NOW AND COLLECT LATER.

NOWHERESVILLE, U.S.A.

GO TO YOUR LOCAL POST OFFICE, PICK UP A CHANGE-OF-ADDRESS FORM, AND FILL IT OUT IN HIS NAME. THE POST OFFICE WILL ROUTE HIS MAIL AROUND HIS HOME TO THE ''NEW'' ADDRESS YOU LIST.

SLICK TRICK

IF THE VICTIM HAS A POOL, POUR A GALLON OF MOTOR OIL IN IT WHILE HE'S AWAY. HE'LL HAVE TO BUY NEW FILTERS, FLUSH HIS LINES AND PUMP, AND COMPLETELY CLEAN OUT THE POOL— AN EXPENSIVE UNDERTAKING.

WHEN HE DRAINS THE POOL, SEE THAT ON THE BOTTOM HE FINDS A TOY, SUNKEN OIL TANKER OF LIBERIAN REGISTRY.

WELL DUN

SEND HIM **PAST DUE** NOTICES FROM VARIOUS DEPARTMENT STORES, SHOPS, ETC., FOR BILLS HE DOESN'T REALLY OWE. HE WILL HAVE TO CALL AND TRY TO GET THE CONFUSION STRAIGHTENED OUT— AND THAT WILL COST HIM MUCH TIME AND TROUBLE.

VICAR-IOUS VISIT

SEND OVER A CLERGYMAN TO:

(1) ADMINISTER LAST RITES TO THE ''DYING'' VICTIM.

(2) SMOOTHE OVER A DOMESTIC SQUABBLE. EXPLAIN THAT YOU THE VICTIM AND YOUR SPOUSE HAVE BEEN FIGHTING ALL NIGHT, AND YOU'RE AFRAID IT'S GOING TO END IN MURDER IF HE DOESN'T INTERVENE.

MANURE CURE

ORDER A LOAD OF MANURE IN HIS NAME. WHILE YOUR ENEMY IS AT WORK, HAVE IT SPREAD ON HIS FRONT YARD, EXPLAINING THAT YOU PLAN TO USE IT AS FERTILIZER.

TERMINAL TAXIS

CALL EVERY TAXI SERVICE IN TOWN AND SEND TAXIS TO THE VICTIM'S HOME THIRTY MINUTES APART ALL NIGHT. REQUEST THAT THE DRIVERS INDICATE THEIR ARRIVAL BY RINGING HIS DOORBELL.

IF YOU DO THIS OFTEN ENOUGH, HE WILL NEVER BE ABLE TO GET A TAXI WHEN HE REALLY NEEDS ONE.

ANTS FROM AN UNCLE

SEND THE VICTIM'S CHILDREN AN ANT FARM, ACCOMPANIED BY A NOTE SAYING THE GIFT IS FROM AN OUT-OF-TOWN UNCLE. BORE A TINY HOLE IN AN INCONSPICUOUS PLACE SO THAT THE ANTS CAN ESCAPE AFTER THE FARM IS INSIDE THE VIC-TIM'S HOME.

DEFOLIANTICS

PAY A VISIT TO THE VICTIM'S PROPERTY LATE AT NIGHT AND CAREFULLY CUT A GROOVE AROUND EACH OF HIS TREES AND BUSHES WITH A POCKET-KNIFE. THIS WILL CAUSE THEM TO DIE, AND IT WILL COST HIM A FORTUNE TO REPLACE THEM.

TWO-FISTED UNLISTED

CALL THE TELEPHONE COMPANY AND HAVE HIS PHONE NUMBER CHANGED TO AN UNLISTED NUMBER. THEY WILL BILL HIM FOR THIS SERVICE. IN ADDITION, WHEN HE CALLS THE COMPANY TO GET HIS NEW NUMBER, THEY WON'T LET HIM HAVE IT.

AD IRRITATUM

PHONE THE ADVERTISING DEPARTMENT OF YOUR LOCAL NEWSPAPER AND PLACE AN AD SIMILAR TO THE FOLLOWING:

FOR SALE BY OWNER: THREE-BEDROOM, TWO-BATH HOME WITH LARGE LAWN. OWNER LEAVING TOWN, MUST SELL FAST. HOUSE IS LOCATED AT _____ , MAY BE SEEN AT ANY TIME.

GIVE THE VICTIM'S NAME AND ADDRESS. BILL THE AD TO HIM. HE'LL HAVE TO ENDURE A STRING OF CURIOUS PEOPLE STOPPING TO INQUIRE ABOUT THE HOUSE.

THE AD TAKER MAY WISH TO VERIFY THE AD, SO GIVE HIM THE NUMBER OF THE PAY PHONE YOU'RE CALLING FROM AND WAIT THERE UNTIL HE CALLS. ADS ARE USUALLY VERIFIED IMMEDIATELY.

CHAPTER TWO
SHATTERING ALLIANCES

PHONE PHUN

(1) GET A GIRL TO CALL THE VICTIM'S HOME AND ASK FOR HIM BY NAME—OR BY A PET NICKNAME (IF YOU KNOW IT) THAT ONLY HIS WIFE CALLS HIM.

(2) CALL HIS HOME—AND IF HIS WIFE ANSWERS, PAUSE BRIEFLY AND THEN HANG UP. SHE'LL THINK A GIRL WAS CALLING FOR HIM.

(3) IF HE ANSWERS, BREATHE HEAVILY IN THE PHONE UNTIL HE HANGS UP. OR LAUGH MANIACALLY.

(4) PHONE HIM AT 3 A.M. EVERY NIGHT FOR A WEEK, WAIT A WEEK AND THEN RESUME THE CALLS.

EVENTUALLY HE'LL BE FORCED TO CHANGE HIS PHONE TO AN UNLISTED NUMBER. BUT HE'LL HAVE TO PAY TO HAVE IT DONE.

SEPTIC SHENANIGANS

GET A FRIEND TO GO TO THE VICTIM'S HOME AND PRETEND HE'S A SALESMAN OF SOME SORT. WHILE HE'S THERE, HAVE HIM GO TO THE BATHROOM AND STUFF A WASHCLOTH FAR DOWN INTO THE COMMODE. THIS WILL CAUSE THE COMMODE TO OVERFLOW BOUNTIFULLY, AND WITHOUT WARNING.

DEPENDING ON THE COMMODE'S DESIGN, IT MAY FLOOD THE WHOLE FIRST FLOOR OF THE VICTIM'S HOUSE.

RESERVATIONS FOR TWO

CALL AND MAKE RESERVATIONS FOR TWO IN THE VICTIM'S NAME AT A HIGH-CLASS MOTEL OUT OF TOWN. GIVE HIS HOME PHONE NUMBER AND REQUEST CONFIRMATION TWO DAYS BEFORE THE RESERVATION DATE.

CALL OR WRITE A TRAVEL AGENCY, BOOK TRIPS FOR TWO IN HIS NAME. BUT INSTEAD OF HIS WIFE'S NAME, LIST HIS SECRETARY'S OR ANOTHER WOMAN'S NAME. HAVE THE ITINERARY MAILED TO HIS HOME.

BRIEF MESSAGE

MAIL THE VICTIM A PAIR OF PANTIES. HAVE THE PACKAGE MARKED "PERSONAL" IN A FEMININE HAND (THIS WILL INTRIGUE HIS WIFE). ENCLOSE A SHORT NOTE: "HOPE THESE REMIND YOU OF US!"

AS A VARIATION, MAIL HIM A PAIR OF SOILED MEN'S BRIEFS. ENCLOSE THE SAME NOTE AS ABOVE.

POSTAL PARANOIA

SEND YOUR VICTIM "HATE MAIL" THAT REALLY ISN'T HATE MAIL AT ALL. SAY THINGS LIKE: "I'LL BE IN TOWN ON JULY 2. WILL CONTACT YOU." LEAVE THE LETTERS UNSIGNED.

IF HE'S THE ONE WHO OPENS THE LETTERS, HE'LL PROBABLY THINK A DERANGED MANIAC IS OUT TO GET HIM. IF HIS SPOUSE INTERCEPTS THEM, SHE'LL THINK THEY'RE FROM ONE OF HIS SECRET GIRLFRIENDS.

THE PHANTOM JEWELER

WHEN YOU VISIT A NEARBY TOWN, MAIL THE VICTIM A POSTCARD READING:

''DEAR MR. _____ ,
    IN CHECKING OVER OUR RECORDS, WE FIND THAT YOU STILL OWE $50 ON THE DIAMOND ENGAGEMENT RING YOU PUR- CHASED LAST JANUARY 8. THIS BILL SHOULD HAVE BEEN PAID MONTHS AGO. PLEASE REMIT THE BALANCE WITHIN 5 DAYS OR WE WILL HAVE NO CHOICE BUT TO TURN THIS OVER TO A COLLECTION AGENCY.

                    SINCERELY,
                    JACKSON'S JEWELERS
                    108 UNION STREET''

    SINCE IT'S A POSTCARD, ODDS ARE THAT THE VICTIM'S SPOUSE WILL READ IT—AND WONDER WHO THE RING WAS FOR.

    INVENT A FICTITIOUS NAME FOR THE JEWELRY STORE. IF THE VICTIM IS THE TYPE WHO WORRIES ABOUT HIS CREDIT RATING, HE'LL TRY TO CALL THE STORE AND STRAIGHTEN OUT THE ERROR . . . AND FAILING TO FIND IT LISTED IN THE YELLOW PAGES, HE'LL HAVE NO CHOICE BUT TO DRIVE TO THE TOWN AND LOOK FOR IT.

KINGSTOWN SALLIE

TYPE OUT THE FOLLOWING LETTER, PLACING
THE VICTIM'S FIRST NAME IN THE BLANKS:

"DEAR SALLIE,
    HELLO, MY NAME IS _____ . I'M
ALWAYS HOT TO TROT AND ENJOY ALL
KINDS OF LOVIN'. I'D REALLY LIKE TO
MEET YOU. YOUR ADVERTISEMENT IN
THE SWINGERS JOURNAL FOR DECEMBER
MAKES YOU SOUND LIKE A HOT LITTLE
ITEM, BUT I'LL BET I COULD PUT OUT
YOUR FIRE. SORRY, BUT I CAN'T SEND YOU
MY TELEPHONE NUMBER, BUT IF YOU ARE
INTERESTED IN GETTING TOGETHER,
PLEASE LET ME KNOW. YOU CAN WRITE
TO ME AT THE ADDRESS ON THIS EN-
VELOPE, BUT BE SURE TO MARK YOUR
LETTER "PERSONAL" SO I'LL GET IT UN-
OPENED. I'M LOOKING FORWARD TO
HEARING FROM YOU.

    FONDLY,

    _____

P.S. I AM WELL BUILT, IF YOU
KNOW WHAT I MEAN."

PUT THE LETTER IN AN ENVELOPE ADDRESSED
TO MISS SALLIE DAVIS, P.O. BOX 1805, KINGS-
TOWN, TENNESSEE. MARK IT "PERSONAL" AND
PLACE THE VICTIM'S NAME AND HOME ADDRESS IN
THE UPPER LEFT-HAND CORNER.

SINCE THERE IS NO KINGSTOWN, TENNESSEE,
THE LETTER WILL BE RETURNED TO THE VICTIM'S
HOME WHERE, HOPEFULLY, HIS WIFE WILL INTER-
CEPT IT.

KNOW THIS MAN?

PLACE AN AD SIMILAR TO THE FOLLOWING IN A
SWINGER'S MAGAZINE (YOU CAN BUY ONE AT ANY
PORNO BOOKSTORE):

"WANTED: CLEAN-CUT YOUNG MEN/WOMEN
INTERESTED IN GREEK, FRENCH, GOLDEN
SHOWERS. I AM HOT AND HORNY, READY
FOR ACTION."

GIVE A FULL DESCRIPTION OF THE VICTIM: AGE,
WEIGHT, HEIGHT, OCCUPATION, CITY. IF YOU HAVE
A PHOTO OF HIM, PLACE IT IN THE AD.

WHEN THE AD APPEARS, MAIL A COPY TO THE
VICTIM'S WIFE AND BOSS, ALONG WITH A BRIEF
NOTE: "KNOW THIS MAN?"

A ROSE BY ANOTHER NAME

HAVE A HUGE, EXPENSIVE BOUQUET OF YELLOW ROSES DELIVERED TO THE VICTIM'S WIFE. CHARGE THEM TO HIM, AND HAVE THE FLORIST ENCLOSE A NOTE SAYING: "BECAUSE I LOVE YOU, DARLING."

THE VICTIM WON'T DARE ADMIT HE DIDN'T SEND THEM—HE'LL HAVE TO PAY FOR THEM.

THE FOLLOWING WEEK, HAVE A BOUQUET OF YELLOW ROSES DELIVERED TO HIS SECRETARY, THE WIFE OF HIS WORST ENEMY, OR HIS EX-WIFE (IF HE HAS ONE). ENCLOSE A NOTE SAYING: "BECAUSE I LOVE YOU, DARLING." HAVE THE BILL AND A COPY OF THE NOTE SENT TO HIS HOME.

MONEYGRAM SCAM

CALL THE VICTIM ON HIS BIRTHDAY, SAY YOU'RE FROM WESTERN UNION AND HAVE A MONEYGRAM FROM HIS AUNT _____ IN _____ . TELL HIM HE'LL HAVE TO COME BY THE OFFICE AND PICK IT UP.

(YOU NEED BACKGROUND SOUNDS A LA WESTERN UNION FOR THIS ONE. EITHER TAPE-RECORD THEM AT A W. U. OFFICE, OR FAKE THEM BY RECORDING THE RAPID CHATTERING AND BELL OF YOUR TYPEWRITER.)

TAPPED RESOURCES

THIS ONE IS FAIRLY COMPLEX—BUT IT CAN DO PLENTY OF DAMAGE TO YOUR VICTIM'S MARRIAGE:

HAVE A SWEET-VOICED YOUNG THING PHONE THE VICTIM, PRETEND SHE HAS A WRONG NUMBER, AND THEN LURE HIM INTO A PROTRACTED CONVERSATION WITH BREATHLESS COME-ONS LIKE: "MY, YOU HAVE A REALLY NICE VOICE." IF THE VICTIM IS HUMAN, HE'LL TALK TO HER UNTIL SHE PUTS DOWN THE PHONE.

TAPE-RECORD THE CALL (YOU CAN BUY A TELEPHONE PICKUP MIKE FOR ABOUT $1.50 AT MOST ELECTRONICS OUTLETS). DURING THE CONVERSATION, HAVE THE GIRL LEAD THE VICTIM INTO SAYING THINGS LIKE: "YES, I LOVE IT, TOO." (HE MIGHT GIVE THIS ANSWER, FOR INSTANCE, IF THE GIRL SAYS: "I WAS JUST GOING OUT FOR A PIZZA. I JUST LOVE IT, DON'T YOU?")

AFTER THE CALL, ERASE THE GIRL'S HARMLESS COMMENTS FROM THE TAPE AND HAVE HER REPLACE THEM WITH DAMNING ONES. FOR EXAMPLE, YOU MIGHT ERASE THE GIRLS' COMMENT ON PIZZA AND SUBSTITUTE "I'LL BET YOUR GOOD AT ORAL SEX. I JUST LOVE IT, DON'T YOU?" (ON TAPE, THE VICTIM WILL THEN OF COURSE, REPLY THAT HE LOVES IT, TOO).

NEXT, MAIL THE ALTERED TAPE, OR A PORTION OF IT, TO THE VICTIM'S WIFE. ENCLOSE A NOTE SAYING YOU'RE THE GIRL'S BOYFRIEND, BECAME SUSPICIOUS THAT SHE WAS PLAYING AROUND, AND PICKED UP THIS CONVERSATION WHILE TAPPING HER PHONE. SUGGEST THAT THE VICTIM'S WIFE PLAY THE TAPE. LISTEN FOR THE FIREWORKS.

HIGH-HEELED SNEAKY

MAIL THE VICTIM'S WIFE A PAIR OF SEQUINED HIGH HEELS. ENCLOSE A LETTER—TYPED ON MOTEL STATIONERY—THAT SAYS:

"DEAR MRS. _____ ,
    WHEN YOU AND YOUR HUSBAND WERE HERE, YOU LEFT THESE SHOES IN YOUR ROOM. WE TRIED TO REACH YOU BY PHONE BUT COULDN'T, SO WE HAVE MAILED THE SHOES INSTEAD. PLEASE REIMBURSE IN THE AMOUNT OF $ ____ FOR MAILING COSTS.

        YOURS TRULY,
        HOWARD COLSON
        DESK CLERK"

THE SHOES, OF COURSE, DO NOT BELONG TO HER. YOU BOUGHT THEM FOR HALF A BUCK AT A USED CLOTHING STORE.

POSTAL PERFIDY

TYPE THE VICTIM'S NAME AND ADDRESS ON LABELS, STICK THEM ON THE SLEAZIEST PORNO-GRAPHIC MAGAZINES YOU CAN FIND, AND MAIL THEM TO THE VICTIM. HOPEFULLY HIS WIFE WILL INTERCEPT THEM AND ASSUME HE'S SUBSCRIBING TO THE DIRTY BOOKS.

REDECORATE

IF THE VICTIM ORDERS ANY FURNITURE, DRAP-
ERIES, ETC., CALL THE COMPANY LATER AND CAN-
CEL THE ORDER—OR CHANGE IT AROUND
COMPLETELY.

IF YOU NOTICE, FOR EXAMPLE, A CARPET COM-
PANY TRUCK PARKED IN FRONT OF HIS HOME,
PHONE THE COMPANY A DAY LATER AND SAY
YOU'VE DECIDED TO GO WITH A DIFFERENT COLOR
OR STYLE OF CARPET. GIVE THE COMPANY
ANOTHER COLOR—OR SAY YOU'LL BE DOWN TO
PICK OUT ANOTHER, THEN DON'T GO.

RUBBER PLANT

DROP A USED RUBBER ON THE REAR FLOORBOARD
OF THE VICTIM'S CAR.

MAIL LUST

SEND THE VICTIM'S NAME AND ADDRESS TO ONE OF THE MULTITUDE OF COMPANIES WHO SELL PORNOGRAPHIC ITEMS BY MAIL. HIS NAME WILL BE PLACED ON A NATIONAL MAILING LIST, AND OTHER FIRMS WILL BOMBARD HIM WITH PORNO BROCHURES. IT'S ALSO LIKELY THE GOVERNMENT, WHICH IS FOND OF KEEPING SECRET LISTS, WILL ADD HIS NAME TO THEIR LIST OF ORDER-BY-MAIL PERVERTS AND HARASS HIM ACCORDINGLY.

LATER, MAIL BATCHES OF SOFT-CORE PORNO PICTURES TO HIS HOME AND OFFICE, ALONG WITH A LETTER SAYING: ''HERE ARE THE PHOTOGRAPHS YOU ORDERED.''

FOLLOW THIS BY SUBSCRIBING IN HIS NAME TO A HOMOSEXUAL MAGAZINE. YOU CAN FIND LISTS OF THESE IN NATIONAL GAY NEWSPAPERS.

HAVANA AFFAIR

SEND THE VICTIM'S SPOUSE A NOTE CONFIDING THAT HE'S HAVING AN AFFAIR WITH A PRETTY CUBAN GIRL IN THE OFFICE. DON'T MENTION THE GIRL'S NAME—JUST SAY YOU THOUGHT THE SPOUSE OUGHT TO KNOW HE'S HOODWINKING HER.

LOW RENT RENDEZVOUS

WRITE THE VICTIM—ON STATIONERY FROM A MOTEL WITH A REPUTATION AS A RENDEZVOUS FOR LOVERS—AND ASK HIM TO RETURN THE KEY TO ROOM 117.

PHONE HIS WIFE, SAY YOU'RE THE DESK CLERK AT THE HAPPY NIGHTS INN AND THAT HE LEFT HIS OVERCOAT IN THE ROOM WHEN HE WAS THERE THE OTHER NIGHT. EXPLAIN THAT YOU GOT HIS HOME PHONE NUMBER FROM A BUSINESS CARD IN THE COAT POCKET. ASK HER TO SEND HIM OVER FOR THE COAT.

CALL THE VICTIM'S SPOUSE, ANGRILY ACCUSING HIM OF PLAYING AROUND WITH YOUR SPOUSE. IF YOU KNOW OF EXACT TIMES HE HAS BEEN AWAY FROM HOME RECENTLY, LIST THOSE AS RENDEZVOUS TIMES. THREATEN VIOLENCE IF THE AFFAIR ISN'T BROKEN OFF IMMEDIATELY. IF YOU'RE A WOMAN, CRY ON THE PHONE AND TALK ABOUT "THE CHILDREN."

CHAPTER THREE
PERSONAL COMBAT

HAPPY BIRTHDAY

ON THE VICTIM'S BIRTHDAY, SEND HIM A BOX OF HOMEMADE CHOCOLATE CHIP COOKIES. ENCLOSE A NOTE READING: "HAPPY BIRTHDAY, GRANDSON," AND SIGN HIS GRANDMOTHER'S NAME. WHEN YOU BAKE THE COOKIES, USE BITS OF EX-LAX INSTEAD OF CHOCOLATE CHIPS.

IF THE VICTIM IS A WOMAN, SEND A GIFT-WRAPPED PACKAGE TO HER PLACE OF EMPLOY-MENT WITH AN ENCLOSED CARD THAT SAYS: "HAPPY BIRTHDAY—HERE'S SOMETHING YOU REALLY NEED." AS HER FELLOW WORKERS CROWD AROUND, SHE'LL UNWRAP IT TO REVEAL—A BOTTLE OF LIQUID DOUCHE.

TERMINAL CANCEL

CALL THE CIRCULATION DEPARTMENT OF YOUR LOCAL NEWSPAPER, BITTERLY COMPLAIN ABOUT A RECENT EDITORIAL, AND ANGRILY CANCEL THE VICTIM'S SUBSCRIPTION.

IF THE VICTIM SUBSCRIBES TO CABLE TV, CALL AND CANCEL THAT, TOO.

IF HE DOESN'T SUBSCRIBE TO EITHER THE NEWSPAPER OR CABLE SERVICE, SIGN HIM UP.

BOSS SLUR

WRITE A CONFIDENTIAL NOTE TIPPING OFF THE VICTIM'S BOSS THAT THE VICTIM HAS BEEN LOUDLY TELLING PALS HIS BOSS IS A FOOL, STUPID, AN ASS, ETC. MOST BOSSES ARE PARANOID, AND THE VICTIM COULD VERY WELL LOSE HIS JOB.

STAND BY

IF YOU KNOW THE VICTIM IS GOING ON A PLANE TRIP, CALL AND CANCEL HIS RESERVATIONS. THIS WORKS ESPECIALLY WELL DURING THE BUSY HOLIDAY SEASON: IT WILL BE ALMOST IMPOSSIBLE FOR HIM TO GET ANOTHER SEAT.

INFERIORITY COMPLEX

IF THE VICTIM HAS PHYSICAL SHORTCOMINGS, MAKE HIM MORE CONSCIOUS OF THEM. IF HE'S OVERWEIGHT FOR EXAMPLE, CUT OUT PICTURES OF FAT PEOPLE, HIPPOS, AND WALRUSES AND MAIL THEM TO HIM. IF HE'S LOSING HAIR, SEND HIM BROCHURES FROM HAIRPIECE MANUFACTURERS.

IF YOU HAVE REASON TO BELIEVE HE'S IMPOTENT, SEND HIM A SMALL TOY TELEPHONE WITH A NOTE READING: "IF YOU CAN'T COME, CALL."

ELEVEN MOST WANTED LIST

GO TO YOUR LOCAL POST OFFICE AND CHECK THE "WANTED" POSTERS. IF ANY FUGITIVE RESEMBLES THE VICTIM, STICK A NOTE ON IT SAYING: "THIS MAN IS LIVING ON _____ STREET UNDER THE FAKE IDENTITY _____ ." LIST THE VICTIM'S ADDRESS AND NAME. SOMEONE WILL BE INTRIGUED ENOUGH TO CALL THE F.B.I.

IF THE VICTIM IS A MEMBER OF A MINORITY OR HAS AN ACCENT, REPORT HIM/HER TO THE IMMIGRATION AND NATURALIZATION OFFICE AS AN ILLEGAL ALIEN.

DEADBEAT

TYPE UP PHONY LETTERS FROM DEPARTMENT STORES CHARGING THAT THE VICTIM NEVER PAYS HIS BILLS. HERE'S A SAMPLE LETTER:

"DEAR SIR:
  THIS IS TO INFORM YOU THAT MR. (VICTIM) OF (ADDRESS) PURCHASED A SET OF 6. 15 X 28 TIRES FROM US LAST AUGUST 12 AND HAS FAILED TO PAY AS PROMISED. MR. _____ HAS MADE ONLY TWO OF THE TWELVE PAYMENTS, AND IS NOW FOUR PAYMENTS IN ARREARS. WE HAVE TURNED THE MATTER OVER TO OUR ATTORNEY FOR COLLECTION.

          SINCERELY,
          CHARLES JOHNSON
          CREDIT MANAGER
          THOMPSON TIRE CO."

IF YOU CAN, PLACE DEPARTMENT STORE LETTERHEADS ON THE LETTERS. MAIL THEM TO YOUR LOCAL CREDIT REPORTING AGENCY, AND WATCH HIS CREDIT RATING DROP.

VOODOO ADIEU

IF THE VICTIM IS HOSPITALIZED, SEND HIM A VOODOO DOLL WITH A PIN PLACED IN THE AREA OF HIS PROBLEM. FOR EXAMPLE, IF HE'S HAVING PROSTATE GLAND SURGERY, YOU KNOW WHERE YOU CAN STICK IT.

A VOODOO DOLL CAN EASILY BE CARVED FROM SOFT WOOD, OR YOU CAN BUY ONE IN ANY NOVELTY SHOP FOR A COUPLE OF BUCKS.

JUST BEFORE THE VICTIM IS RELEASED FROM THE HOSPITAL, CALL A FLORIST SHOP AND HAVE A FUNERAL WREATH SENT TO HIS HOME. BILL IT TO HIS EMPLOYER.

NERVOUS SERVICE

WHILE THE VICTIM IS ATTENDING RELIGIOUS SERVICES, PHONE THE CHURCH AND TELL WHOEVER ANSWERS THAT YOU URGENTLY NEED TO TALK TO THE VICTIM. AN USHER WILL ENTER THE CHURCH AND QUIETLY INFORM THE VICTIM—BUT BEFORE HE GETS TO THE PHONE, HANG UP. HE'LL WONDER THROUGHOUT THE REST OF THE SERVICE WHAT THE "EMERGENCY" IS

ERROR PARENT

IF THE VICTIM'S WIFE IS PREGNANT, PHONE HIM AND SAY: "THE CHILD YOUR WIFE IS CARRYING ISN'T YOURS." QUICKLY HANG UP.

HOT PLASTIC

FIND OUT WHAT CHARGE CARDS THE VICTIM HAS, AND:

(1) REPORT THEM STOLEN. GIVE A DESCRIPTION OF THE SUSPECTED THIEF WHICH MATCHES THE VICTIM.

(2) SEND A LETTER TO THE CREDIT CARD COMPANY SAYING YOU WANT TO CANCEL YOUR CARD. EXPLAIN THAT YOU WOULD HAVE MAILED IN THE CARD, BUT YOU LOST IT.

ROADSIDE ATTRACTIONS

WATCH FOR SMALL DEAD ANIMALS—DOGS, CATS, MICE, ETC.—IN THE ROAD. PICK THESE UP, WRAP THEM AND HAVE THEM DELIVERED TO THE VICTIM'S HOME.

IF YOU PLACE THEM IN AN AIRTIGHT CONTAINER, WAIT A WEEK BEFORE HAVING THEM DELIVERED. THIS GIVES THE VICTIM THE BENEFIT OF ALL THAT RICH, FULL-BODIED AROMA.

SECRET STORM

IF YOU KNOW SOMETHING THE VICTIM WANTS TO KEEP SECRET—FOR EXAMPLE, THAT HE CHEATED A FRIEND ON A BUSINESS DEAL, OR CHEATED ON HIS WIFE—WRITE OR CALL THE PEOPLE INVOLVED AND TELL THEM ABOUT IT.

HOLIDAY SPIRIT

TWO WEEKS BEFORE CHRISTMAS, FILL OUT A CHANGE OF ADDRESS CARD IN THE VICTIM'S NAME AND MAIL IT TO THE LOCAL POST OFFICE. LIST THE ADDRESS OF A LOCAL SALVATION ARMY BRANCH AS HIS NEW ADDRESS. THEN CALL THE SALVATION ARMY, GIVE THE VICTIM'S NAME, AND TELL THEM YOU'RE HAVING YOUR CHRISTMAS GIFTS ROUTED DIRECTLY TO THEM.

MAIL ODOR

ORDER A TURD SENT TO THE VICTIM THROUGH THE MAIL. AN ADVERTISEMENT IN "SCREW" MAGAZINE RECENTLY OFFERED THIS SERVICE FOR $10.

(THIS IS AN AMERICAN CLASSIC, AND IS ALSO A FAVORITE IN FRANCE WHERE IT'S KNOWN AS THE "BOITE DE MERDE" [BOX OF FECES]).

NO SALE

IF THE VICTIM ADVERTISES SOMETHING FOR SALE, CALL AND OFFER HIM A RIDICULOUSLY HIGH PRICE FOR IT. EXPLAIN THAT IT'S SOMETHING YOU'VE ALWAYS WANTED. ASK HIM TO HOLD IT FOR FOUR DAYS, TURNING DOWN ALL OTHER OFFERS, UNTIL YOU CAN ROUND UP THE MONEY. AFTER THE FOUR DAYS ARE UP, DROP HIM A NOTE REVEALING THAT YOU PURPOSELY QUEERED HIS SALE.

CHECKUP SETUP

MAKE APPOINTMENTS FOR THE VICTIM WITH DOCTORS, DENTISTS, LAWYERS, AND PSYCHIATRISTS. MANY OF THESE PROFESSIONALS CHARGE FOR VISITS EVEN IF NO ONE SHOWS UP.

IF YOU KNOW THE NAMES OF THE VICTIM'S PERSONAL DOCTOR, DENTIST, ETC., SET UP THE APPOINTMENTS WITH THEM. THIS WILL MAKE IT TOUGH FOR THE VICTIM TO SEE THEM WHEN HE REALLY NEEDS TO.

ALL WORK AND NO PLAY

WHILE THE VICTIM'S SPOUSE IS AWAY FROM HOME, CALL HIM AT WORK AND:

(1) IN AN EXCITED VOICE, TELL HIM WATER IS GUSHING OUT FROM UNDER THE FRONT DOOR OF HIS HOME.

(2) TELL HIM YOU SAW SMOKE COMING OUT A WINDOW.

(3) CONFIDE THAT YOU SAW HIS WIFE AND ANOTHER MAN CHECK INTO THE NO-TELL MOTEL.

AYE, THERE'S THE RUB

MAKE LONG-DISTANCE CALLS TO MASSAGE PARLORS, DATING AND ESCORT SERVICES. TELL THE OPERATOR YOU WANT TO BILL THE CALLS TO YOUR HOME PHONE, AND GIVE HER THE VICTIM'S NUMBER. TALK AS LONG AS YOU CAN, AND ASK THE PLACE TO SEND ANY BROCHURES IT HAS TO THE VICTIM'S HOME. HE'LL HAVE WHOPPING PHONE BILLS—AND ALSO WILL HAVE TO EXPLAIN TO HIS SPOUSE WHY HE WAS CALLING THOSE PLACES.

HANGING ON
THE TELEPHONE

ANY TIME YOU'RE OUT OF TOWN, PLACE A LONG-DISTANCE COLLECT CALL TO THE VICTIM'S HOME. HAVE THE OPERATOR SAY THAT IT'S HIS BROTHER JOHN OR SISTER JANE CALLING (YOU'LL HAVE TO KNOW THESE NAMES). WHEN HE ACCEPTS THE CALL, PUT DOWN THE PAY PHONE AND WALK AWAY.

CHAPTER FOUR
TAKING THE FIGHT
TO THE STREETS

GAY BARB

WRITE A LETTER TO THE EDITOR OF THE LOCAL NEWSPAPER SAYING:

"WHY AREN'T THERE MORE GAY BARS IN THIS TOWN? I'M NOT A HOMOSEXUAL MYSELF, BUT I'VE GOT PLENTY OF FRIENDS WHO ARE, AND I THINK IT'S A SHAME THEY DON'T HAVE MORE PLACES TO GET TOGETHER," ETC.

SIGN THE VICTIM'S NAME AND ADDRESS.

GHOST WRITER

WRITE LETTERS IN YOUR VICTIM'S NAME TO EVERYONE HE KNOWS—NEIGHBORS, FRIENDS IN OTHER TOWNS, ETC.—AND COMPLAIN ABOUT VARIOUS THINGS. FOR EXAMPLE, WRITE HIS FRIEND HARRY AND CALL HIM A "DEADBEAT" FOR NOT RETURNING A FICTITIOUS $10 LOANED YEARS AGO. TYPE YOUR LETTERS AND GET SOMEBODY ELSE TO DO THE SIGNATURES.

HE'LL GET ALL SORTS OF ANGRY CALLS AND LETTERS BACK, AND WILL HAVE TO TAKE THE TIME AND TROUBLE TO EXPLAIN THAT HE DIDN'T SEND THE LETTERS IN THE FIRST PLACE. ALL THIS ADDS UP TO MORE HARASSMENT OF YOUR VICTIM.

FUNEREAL FUN

GET A GIRL TO CALL A LOCAL FUNERAL HOME AND SAY SHE WANTS TO MAKE FUNERAL ARRANGEMENTS FOR HER LATE HUSBAND, WHO WAS KILLED IN A CAR ACCIDENT IN ANOTHER CITY. HAVE HER ASK THE PARLOR TO SEND A MAN TO DISCUSS THE ARRANGEMENTS WITH HER. GIVE THE VICTIM'S ADDRESS.

PHONE THE VICTIM'S OBITUARY IN TO YOUR LOCAL NEWSPAPER. TELL THEM YOU'RE FROM _____ FUNERAL HOME. MOST NEWSPAPERS TAKE THESE OVER THE PHONE WITHOUT QUESTION.

FOLLOW THE FORMAT OF AN OBITUARY CLIPPED FROM THE PAPER.

A.P.B.

IF YOU SEE THE VICTIM DRIVE AWAY FROM HOME OR HIS OFFICE, CALL THE AUTHORITIES AND REPORT YOUR CAR STOLEN. DESCRIBE HIS AUTO AND REPORT THE DIRECTION HE'S HEADING.

IF YOU KNOW HE'S BEEN DRINKING—FOR EXAMPLE, IF YOU SAW HIM IN A BAR—REPORT HIM AS A DRUNK DRIVER. TELL THE AUTHORITIES HE ALMOST RAN YOU OFF THE ROAD.

BADMOUTH

CALL THE VICTIM'S TOUGHEST NEIGHBOR, TELL HIM YOU WORK DOWN AT THE LOCAL BAR (OR RESTAURANT OR GARAGE) AND THAT THE VICTIM HAS BEEN DOWN THERE BADMOUTHING HIM.

IF YOU KNOW OF A SPECIFIC SQUABBLE BETWEEN VICTIM AND NEIGHBOR, SAY THE VICTIM WAS DISCUSSING THAT WHEN HE MADE HIS UNCOMPLIMENTARY REMARKS. TELL THE NEIGHBOR YOU DIDN'T REALLY WANT TO GET INVOLVED, "BUT I DON'T THINK ANYBODY SHOULD BE TALKED ABOUT THE WAY HE TALKED ABOUT YOU. . ."

PERVERT ALERT

IF THE VICTIM COACHES A LITTLE LEAGUE TEAM, OR IS INVOLVED WITH YOUNGSTERS IN ANY WAY, ANONYMOUSLY INFORM THE FATHER OF ONE OF THE BOYS THAT THE VICTIM HAS BEEN MAKING ADVANCES TOWARD THE BOY. CHOOSE THE ROUGHEST REDNECK YOU KNOW.

IF THE VICTIM TAKES REGULAR WALKS, CALL ONE OF HIS NEIGHBORS AND ANGRILY REPORT THAT HE'S ''FLASHING'' CHILDREN. TELL THEM YOU'RE A PASSING MOTORIST WHO WITNESSED HIS DISGUSTING, PERVERTED ACT.

TACK UP NOTICES AROUND THE NEIGHBORHOOD SAYING HE'S A HOMOSEXUAL, CROSS-DRESSER OR CHILD MOLESTER. GIVE SPECIFIC DATES, TIMES (FICTITIOUS, OF COURSE) WHEN HE'S COMMITTED THESE OFFENSES. MOST OF HIS NEIGHBORS WILL KNOW THE NOTICES ARE FAKE—BUT SOME WILL BELIEVE THEY'RE TRUE AND WILL AVOID HIM OR TREAT HIM AS A CRIMINAL.

DOOR TO DOOR DILEMMA

IF THE VICTIM IS A DOOR-TO-DOOR SALESMAN, FOLLOW HIM TO THE NEIGHBORHOOD WHERE HE'S WORKING THAT DAY. THEN CALL POLICE, SAY YOU'RE A RESIDENT OF THAT NEIGHBORHOOD, AND COMPLAIN THAT HE'S BOTHERING YOU OR EVEN THREATENING YOU. DESCRIBE HIM AND HIS CAR TO THE COPS.

MANLY MISCHIEF

SCRAWL THE VICTIM'S NAME AND PHONE
NUMBER ON BATHROOM WALLS ALL OVER TOWN,
ESPECIALLY IN GAY BARS. SAY HE'S AVAILABLE TO
PERFORM VARIOUS SEXUAL ACTS ON MEN.

PAINT IT BLACK

CALL A TOWING SERVICE AND HAVE THE VIC-
TIM'S CAR TOWED TO A GARAGE FOR A TUNEUP OR
PAINT JOB. GIVE A FICTITIOUS NAME SO HE'LL
HAVE A TOUGH TIME TRACKING DOWN HIS AUTO.

YOU'RE MORE LIKELY TO PULL THIS OFF IF YOU
CAN CASUALLY TELL THE TOWING SERVICE: "THE
KEYS ARE IN MY CAR" (WALK BY AND CHECK) AND
REEL OFF THE LICENSE NUMBER.

HIT AND MISSIVE

IF YOU SEE A PARKED CAR THAT'S BEEN DENTED,
AND THE OFFENDING DRIVER HAS LEFT HIS NAME
AND ADDRESS ON A NOTE ON THE WINDSHIELD,
REPLACE IT WITH A NOTE BEARING THE VICTIM'S
NAME AND ADDRESS.

TO CATCH A THIEF

IF YOU SEE THE VICTIM ENTER A DEPARTMENT STORE, FOLLOW HIM INSIDE. CASUALLY APPROACH A YOUNG FLOOR CLERK (YOUNG ONES ARE MORE GULLIBLE) AND SAY: "LISTEN, I DON'T WANT TO GET INVOLVED, BUT THAT GUY OVER THERE JUST STUCK SOME MERCHANDISE IN HIS POCKET." AS STORE SECURITY PERSONNEL ZERO IN ON HIM, BUY SOMETHING SMALL AND LEAVE—THEN DROP IT IN THE VICTIM'S CAR OUTSIDE THE STORE. SECURITY PEOPLE OFTEN SEARCH SUSPECTED SHOPLIFTERS' CARS, TOO. EVEN IF THEY DON'T FIND THE ITEM, THE VICTIM WILL WONDER HOW IT GOT IN HIS CAR.

OUT TO LUNCH

WHILE THE VICTIM IS DINING OUT OR WATCHING A MOVIE WITH HIS WIFE OR GIRLFRIEND, LEAVE A NOTE ON HIS CAR WINDSHIELD SAYING: "HI, DOLL! RECOGNIZED YOUR CAR, BUT COULDN'T WAIT FOR YOU. STILL SEEING YOU FRIDAY, RIGHT? LUV YA—SHERRI."

PLACE THE NOTE ON THE PASSENGER SIDE. WRITE LARGE ENOUGH SO THAT ANYONE CAN EASILY READ IT.

MINOR INCIDENT

SEND THE VICTIM'S BOSS AN ANONYMOUS LETTER SAYING:

(A) YOU SAW THE VICTIM TRYING TO PICK UP GIRLS AT A LOCAL ELEMENTARY SCHOOL, AND THOUGHT THE BOSS OUGHT TO KNOW ABOUT IT BEFORE THE MAN GETS ARRESTED AND SHAMES THE COMPANY.

(B) THE VICTIM HAS HERPES III AND COULD CONTAMINATE THE WHOLE OFFICE IF HE'S ALLOWED TO USE THE COMMODES IN THE COMPANY BATHROOMS.

BRAT CHAT

PHONE THE VICTIM JUST AFTER SCHOOL HOURS, SAY YOU'RE THE PRINCIPAL OF HIS CHILD'S SCHOOL AND NEED TO DISCUSS AN IMPORTANT DISCIPLINARY PROBLEM WITH HIM. MAKE AN APPOINTMENT TO SEE HIM AT THE SCHOOL AT 8 A.M. THE NEXT DAY.

SICK CALL

IF THE VICTIM CALLS IN SICK, CALL HIS OFFICE A COUPLE OF HOURS LATER AND SAY YOU SAW HIM AT THE BEACH OR A MOVIE.

SPYMASTER (BAITER)

PLACE COMPANY-OWNED DOCUMENTS OR MATE-
RIALS IN THE POCKETS OF THE VICTIM'S JACKET,
OR IN HIS CAR, THEN TIP OFF COMPANY OFFICIALS
HE'S STEALING FROM THE COMPANY OR SPYING
FOR ANOTHER FIRM.

COMPANY MAN

PUT OUT A "NEWS RELEASE" ANNOUNCING THE VICTIM'S APPOINTMENT TO A POST WITH A RIVAL FIRM. SUPPOSE, FOR EXAMPLE, THAT HE WORKS FOR JOHNSON ENTERPRISES, A RIVAL OF THOR INDUSTRIES. YOUR RELEASE WOULD READ SOMETHING LIKE THIS:

NEWS RELEASE
FOR IMMEDIATE RELEASE

"JOHN BROWN, PRESIDENT OF THOR INDUSTRIES, ANNOUNCED TODAY THAT JOE VICTIM HAS BEEN APPOINTED CHIEF OF QUALITY CONTROL FOR THE COMPANY.

MR. VICTIM, 39, WAS PREVIOUSLY EMPLOYED AS ASSISTANT CHIEF OF QUALITY CONTROL FOR JOHNSON ENTERPRISES. HE IS MARRIED TO THE FORMER KATHY DAVIS AND THEY HAVE TWO CHILDREN, JOHN, JR., 8, AND LEROY, 7. MR. VICTIM IS A MEMBER OF THE KNIGHTS OF THE SQUARE TABLE AND ELKS LODGE 108."

MAKE THE RELEASE FIVE TO SIX PARAGRAPHS LONG, PLACE A LETTERHEAD FROM THOR INDUSTRIES AT ITS TOP, AND PHOTOCOPY THE COMBINATION. MAIL COPIES TO ALL LOCAL NEWSPAPERS.

MOST NEWSPAPERS ROUTINELY PRINT SUCH
ANNOUNCEMENTS WITHOUT CHECKING THEIR
AUTHENTICITY, SO IT'S A SURE BET THAT SOME OF
THE RELEASES WILL WIND UP IN PRINT. THE VIC-
TIM WILL, OF COURSE, DENY HE'S LEAVING JOHN-
SON INDUSTRIES, BUT HIS BOSS WILL NO DOUBT
WONDER IF SOME PUBLIC RELATIONS MAN DIDN'T
MAIL OUT THE RELEASE PREMATURELY.

WHILE YOU
WERE AWAY . . .

WHILE THE VICTIM IS ON VACATION:

(1) CALL THE PERSONNEL DEPARTMENT WHERE
HE WORKS AND TELL THEM YOU QUIT. SAY YOU'VE
FOUND A BETTER JOB AND WON'T BE BACK. GIVE
THEM HIS NAME.

(2) CALL HIS BOSS AND REPORT THAT HE'S BEEN
KILLED IN AN ACCIDENT. SAY YOU'RE A RELATIVE.

(3) MOVE HIS PROPERTY MARKERS, OR REMOVE
THEM ENTIRELY. IF HE EVER DECIDES TO BUILD A
FENCE, HE'LL HAVE TO HAVE HIS LOT
RESURVEYED.

BOSSITIS

CALL THE VICTIM'S BOSS AND:

(1) TELL HIM YOU'RE WITH THE COLLECTION DEPARTMENT OF A LARGE STORE AND HAVE A BAD CHECK FROM THE VICTIM. TELL HIM YOU'VE BEEN TRYING FOR A WEEK TO COLLECT YOUR MONEY, BUT THE VICTIM HAS IGNORED YOUR CALLS. THREATEN COURT ACTION IF THE CHECK ISN'T PICKED UP BY 5 P.M. THAT DAY. SOUND EXASPER-ATED. THE BOSS WILL THINK THE VICTIM IS A DEADBEAT.

(2) CONFIDE THAT YOU'RE WITH THE PERSONNEL DEPARTMENT OF ANOTHER FIRM AND THAT HE'S APPLIED FOR A JOB THERE. ASK THE BOSS WHAT SORT OF EMPLOYEE THE VICTIM IS—WHETHER HE'S RELIABLE, TRUSTWORTHY, ETC.

HIRE THE EX-CON

CALL THE VICTIM'S BOSS AND, IN AN OFFICIAL-SOUNDING VOICE, SAY YOU'RE VERIFYING HIS EMPLOYMENT. GIVE THE IMPRESSION, WITHOUT ACTUALLY SAYING SO, THAT YOU'RE A PROBATION OFFICER AND THAT THE VICTIM HAS BEEN CON-VICTED OF AN UNSPEAKABLE CRIME . . . CHILD-MOLESTING OR SOMETHING TO THAT EFFECT.

EXECUTIVE ACTION

TYPE UP A LETTER TO THE VICTIM FROM A RIVAL FIRM, SAYING SOMETHING LIKE THE FOLLOWING:

_____ , 19____

"DEAR MR. _____ ,

I AM PLEASE TO INFORM YOU THAT WE ARE INDEED INTERESTED IN DISCUSSING FURTHER WITH YOU THE POSSIBILITY OF EMPLOYMENT WITH OUR FIRM. WE FEEL YOU CAN BRING MANY VALUABLE IDEAS AND TECHNIQUES, INCLUDING THOSE YOU MENTIONED AT OUR INITIAL SESSION LAST WEEK, FROM YOUR COMPANY TO OURS. YOU MAY BE ASSURED THAT WE WILL EXERCISE ABSOLUTE DISCRETION IN CASE. PLEASE TELEPHONE ME FOR AN APPOINTMENT AT YOUR CONVENIENCE.

SINCERELY,
J. HARVEY JOHNSON
DIRECTOR OF PERSONNEL"

PLACE THE COMPANY'S LETTERHEAD AT THE TOP OF THIS LETTER, XEROX THE COMBINATION, AND SEND THE COPY TO THE VICTIM'S BOSS. TELL THE BOSS YOU FELT HE SHOULD KNOW THE VICTIM IS SHOPPING AROUND FOR A NEW JOB.

LOUSE OF ILL-REPUTE

IF THE VICTIM HAS A BUSINESS THAT DEALS DIRECTLY WITH THE PUBLIC—FOR EXAMPLE, AN AUTO REPAIR SHOP—PUT UP NOTES ON BULLETIN BOARDS AROUND TOWN WARNING PEOPLE IT'S A RIPOFF OUTFIT.

MYSTERIOUS MESSAGES

WHILE HE'S AT LUNCH, CALL HIS OFFICE AND ASK FOR HIM. WHEN THE PERSON WHO ANSWERS THE PHONE TELLS YOU HE ISN'T IN, ASK THEM TO TAKE A MESSAGE: ''TELL HIM DR. BROWN'S OFFICE CALLED, AND HIS NEW DENTURES ARE READY.'' THIS WILL EMBARRASS HIM, AND HE'LL ALSO HAVE TO CHECK WITH ''DR. BROWN'' TO SEE WHAT'S GOING ON.

AS A VARIATION, SAY YOU'RE A DRUGGIST. EXPLAIN THAT HE BOUGHT TWO TUBES OF PREPARATION ''H'' AT YOUR STORE, THEN RAN OFF AND FORGOT THEM.

LETTER BOMBAST

TYPE UP A BRIEF NOTE LAMBASTING THE VIC-
TIM'S BOSS ("I'D JUST LIKE YOU TO KNOW THAT
YOU'RE A LOW-DOWN S.O.B.," ETC.). INSERT IT IN
AN ENVELOPE—THEN ADDRESS THE ENVELOPE TO
THE BOSS IN THE VICTIM'S OWN HANDWRITING
(YOU'LL NEED A SAMPLE OF HIS WRITING FOR
THIS). IF THE BOSS GETS MAD ENOUGH, HE'LL TRY
TO MATCH THE HANDWRITING TO PEOPLE HE
KNOWS—AND ODDS ARE THAT HE'LL ZERO IN ON
THE VICTIM.

FALSE ALARM

CALL THE VICTIM AT WORK AND TELL HIM HIS
WIFE HAS BEEN BADLY INJURED IN A CAR ACCI-
DENT. PRETEND YOU'RE A HOSPITAL EMERGENCY
ROOM CLERK AND TELL HIM TO RUSH RIGHT OVER.
HE'LL PROBABLY BE SO UPSET THAT HE'LL LEAVE
HIS JOB AND HURRY TO THE HOSPITAL WITHOUT
FIRST PHONING HOME TO SEE IF HIS WIFE IS OKAY.

B³ = 0

IF THE VICTIM RUNS HIS OWN BUSINESS, REPEATEDLY REPORT HIM TO THE BETTER BUSINESS BUREAU AS A CHEAT AND A CROOK. GET DIFFERENT PEOPLE TO COMPLAIN, IF YOU CAN. THIS SHOULD RUIN HIS BUSINESS REPUTATION.

IF THE VICTIM DEALS WITH THE PUBLIC (SALESMAN, WAITER, ETC.) CALL HIS BOSS AND COMPLAIN THAT YOU WERE TREATED SHABBILY BY HIM. ACCUSE THE VICTIM OF BEING DISCOURTEOUS INCOMPETENT, THIEVING, ETC. GET OTHER PEOPLE TO CALL AND COMPLAIN ABOUT THE SAME THING.

GO TO A RIVAL FIRM OF THE VICTIM'S PLACE OF EMPLOYMENT, AND FILL OUT A JOB APPLICATION IN THE VICTIM'S NAME. AT THE POINT WHERE THE APPLICATION ASKS: ''DO WE HAVE YOUR PERMISSION TO CONTACT YOUR PRESENT EMPLOYER?'' CHECK ''YES.'' UNDER ''REFERENCES,'' LIST HIS WORST ENEMIES IN THE OFFICE.

STOOD UP

IF THE VICTIM IS A SALESMAN, HAVE PEOPLE CALL AND MAKE BOGUS APPOINTMENTS TO MEET HIM AT VARIOUS PLACES—RESTAURANTS, CLUBS, ETC. TO KEEP HIM WAITING LONGER, HAVE THEM LEAVE A MESSAGE SAYING THEY WERE DELAYED AND WILL BE HALF AN HOUR LATE.

CHAPTER FIVE

BRINGING UP THE HEAVY ARTILLERY

TAXING PROBLEMS

CALL THE INTERNAL REVENUE SERVICE, TELL THEM THE VICTIM HAS BEEN BOASTING AT WORK ABOUT CHEATING ON HIS TAXES. HINT THAT HE HAS A LUCRATIVE BUSINESS ON THE SIDE BUT DOESN'T REPORT THE EXTRA INCOME. SAY YOU'RE TURNING HIM IN AS A "GOOD CITIZEN," BUT WILL TAKE THE REWARD. IF THE IRS ASKS YOU TO IDENTIFY YOURSELF, GIVE THE NAME AND ADDRESS OF YOUR SECOND-WORST ENEMY.

CALL THE VICTIM, TELL HIM YOU'RE MR. SCHWARTZ WITH THE INTERNAL REVENUE SERVICE AND ARE AUDITING HIS ACCOUNT FOR THE YEAR 1975. ASK HIM TO PLEASE BRING HIS RECORDS FOR THAT YEAR TO THE I.R.S. OFFICE AT 8 A.M. THE FOLLOWING MORNING. GIVE HIM THE ACTUAL ADDRESS OF THE OFFICE.

(ONE YEAR AFTER THIS TRICK WAS PULLED ON A FACTORY WORKER IN WEST PALM BEACH, THE I.R.S. ACTUALLY DID CALL AND TELL HIM HE WAS BEING AUDITED. HE ANGRILY HUNG UP ON THEM . . . AND BOUGHT HIMSELF A PACK OF TROUBLE.)

THINK PINK

APPLY FOR TRAVEL VISAS—IN THE VICTIM'S NAME—AT THE WASHINGTON, D.C., EMBASSIES OF COMMUNIST COUNTRIES SUCH AS ALBANIA AND BULGARIA. EXPLAIN THAT YOU'RE INTERESTED IN EMIGRATING THERE BECAUSE YOU'RE SICK OF THE OPPRESSIVENESS IN AMERICA. HAVE THE VISA INFORMATION SENT TO THE VICTIM'S PLACE OF EMPLOYMENT.

PAPER MURDER

IF YOU CAN OBTAIN A COPY OF A DEATH CERTIF-ICATE, FILL IT OUT IN THE VICTIM'S NAME AND MAIL TO THE U.S. SOCIAL SECURITY OFFICE IN WASHINGTON, D.C. THIS WILL ENTANGLE HIM IN A SNARL OF PROBLEMS WHEN IT COMES TIME FOR HIM TO APPLY FOR SOCIAL SECURITY.

SEND A SECOND COPY TO YOUR COUNTY'S REGIS-TRAR OF VOTERS, AND ASK THEM TO REMOVE HIS NAME FROM THE VOTING LIST.

UNWILLING ACTIVIST

REGISTER THE VICTIM WITH THE COMMUNIST PARTY, RADICAL POLITICAL GROUPS AND HOMO-SEXUAL ORGANIZATIONS. BROCHURES WILL BE SENT TO HIS HOME AND OFFICE, AND HIS NAME WILL GO ON VARIOUS SECRET GOVERNMENT LISTS . . . NONE OF WHICH WILL DO HIM ANY GOOD.

JUST A CONCERNED CITIZEN

IF THE MAN IS VIOLATING ANY LOCAL, STATE OR FEDERAL LAW—BY BURNING LEAVES OUTSIDE, FOR EXAMPLE, OR REMODELING HIS HOME WITHOUT A PERMIT—CALL THE PROPER AUTHORITIES AND REPORT HIM.

LIKEWISE, IF HE HAS ANY OUTSIDE INCOME ON WHICH HE ISN'T PAYING TAXES, REPORT HIM TO THE INTERNAL REVENUE SERVICES. BE ALERT FOR THIS POSSIBILITY—MOST PEOPLE EARN AT LEAST A FEW HUNDRED BUCKS A YEAR AT ODD JOBS, AND NEVER REPORT THAT INCOME.

FRIENDLY
NEIGHBORHOOD PUSHER

CALL YOUR LOCAL "HEROIN HOTLINE" (OR A
SIMILAR AGENCY) AND REPORT THE VICTIM AS A
DRUG DEALER. TELL THEM HE STASHES HIS
SUPPLY IN A SECRET COMPARTMENT IN HIS DEN
WALL.

SYPHILITIC CRITIC

CALL YOUR CITY'S V.D. HOTLINE, AND SAY YOU
CAUGHT YOUR SYPHILIS FROM THE VICTIM.
THEY'LL SEND AN INVESTIGATOR TO QUIZ HIM
ABOUT HIS SEXUAL CONTACTS.

IF THERE'S NO HOTLINE IN YOUR AREA, CALL
THE COUNTY HEALTH DEPARTMENT. TELL THEM A
DOCTOR HAS CONFIRMED THAT YOU HAVE VD, AND
THE VICTIM IS THE ONLY PERSON WITH WHOM
YOU'VE BEEN INTIMATE. EXPLAIN THAT YOU'RE
ASHAMED TO CONTACT THE VICTIM YOURSELF, BUT
YOU FEEL SOMEONE SHOULD TELL HIM HE'S
DISEASED.

AGRICULTURAL AID

TOSS MARIJUANA SEEDS IN THE VICTIM'S SHRUBBERY. WAIT FOUR WEEKS AND TIP OFF THE AUTHORITIES.

ABUSE RUSE

IF YOU SPOT AN ACCIDENTAL CUT OR BRUISE ON ANY OF THE VICTIM'S CHILDREN, REPORT HIM TO THE AUTHORITIES FOR CHILD ABUSE. MANY CITIES HAVE CHILD ABUSE HOTLINES, AND EVERY CALL PROMPTS AN IN-DEPTH INVESTIGATION. THE HOTLINE RECEPTIONIST SELDOM ASKS YOUR NAME.

YOU CAN ALSO REPORT THE VICTIM TO THE A.S.P.C.A. FOR MISTREATING ANIMALS. SAY HE HAS A FEMALE CHIHUAHUA, AND IMPLY THAT HE'S INTO BESTIALITY.

MOONLIGHTER

IF THE VICTIM IS UNEMPLOYED AND COLLECTING COMPENSATION, CALL THE UNEMPLOYMENT BUREAU AND REPORT THAT HE'S MAKING $100 A WEEK PAINTING HOUSES AND ISN'T REPORTING THE INCOME. HE'LL BE QUIZZED, POSSIBLY INVESTIGATED.

SWEET DREAMS

LATE AT NIGHT, AFTER THE VICTIM AND HIS FAMILY HAVE GONE TO BED, CALL THE AUTHORITIES AND REPORT:

(1) THAT YOU SAW A MAN SNEAKING AROUND HIS HOME. GIVE A GENERAL PHYSICAL DESCRIPTION WHICH MATCHES THE VICTIM.

(2) THAT YOU HEARD GUNSHOTS AND SCREAMS COMING FROM HIS HOME.

ASININE PROBE

IF THE VICTIM IS VACATIONING OUTSIDE THE U.S., FIND OUT WHERE AND WHEN HE'LL RE-ENTER THE COUNTRY AND INFORM THE U.S. CUSTOMS OFFICE THERE THAT HE'S BRINGING NARCOTICS BACK INTO THE COUNTRY . . . HIDDEN INSIDE A PLASTIC BAG STUFFED UP HIS REAR END. THEY'LL LAUNCH AN IMMEDIATE ''PROBE.''

GUERRILLA WARFARE

THEN, OF COURSE, FOR YOU BRAVER SOULS THERE ARE THESE DIRECT STRIKES AT THE ENEMY:

1. POUR SUGAR IN HIS CAR'S GAS TANK. THIS WILL DESTROY THE ENGINE.

2. SHOVE A POTATO UP THE EXHAUST PIPE. HE WON'T BE ABLE TO GET THE CAR STARTED.

3. TOSS TACKS UNDER HIS TIRES.

4. BUY A SMALL CAN OF HOT PINK SPRAY PAINT, AND DECORATE THE SIDE OF HIS CAR AT NIGHT.

5. REMOVE THE PICKUP TAGS FROM HIS GAR-BAGE CANS.

6. IF HE HAS A POOL, DUMP YELLOW DYE IN IT AND THEN SEND HIM A NOTE SAYING YOU SAW A GIGANTIC ST. BERNARD PEEING IN THE POOL.